The Good Samaritan

Storyline **Carol Fay Nicks**
Illustrations **Steven Butler**

One day a lawyer asked Jesus a question. "What must I do to be saved?"

"What does the law say you should do?" Jesus asked.

"You should love the Lord your God with all your heart," the lawyer replied, "and love your neighbor as yourself."

"Good answer," Jesus said. "If you do this, you will have eternal life."

But the lawyer did not love some kinds of people, so he asked, "Who is my neighbor?"

Jesus did not answer directly. Instead, he told the lawyer a story.

Once a traveler was making a trip from Jerusalem to Jericho. Along the way, the road went through a wild, rocky ravine.

Just as the man entered the ravine, a robber jumped out from behind a rock and attacked him.

"Help! Help!" cried the traveler. But there was no one near to hear him.

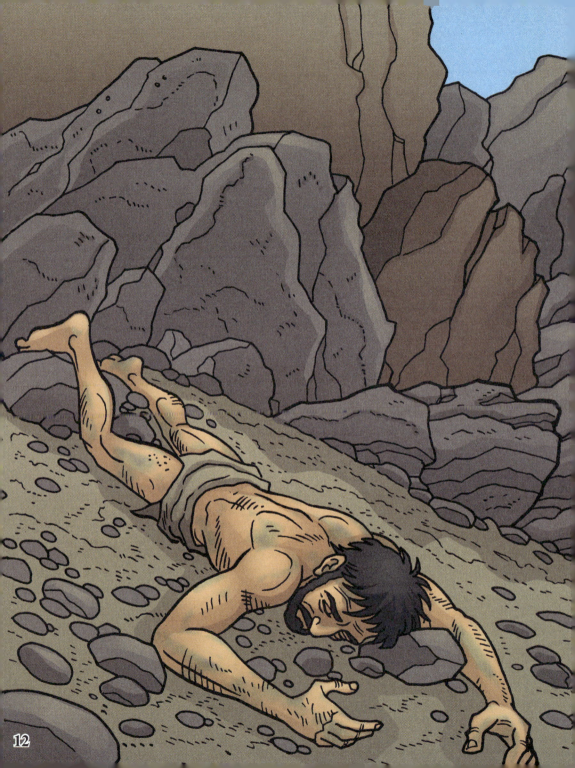

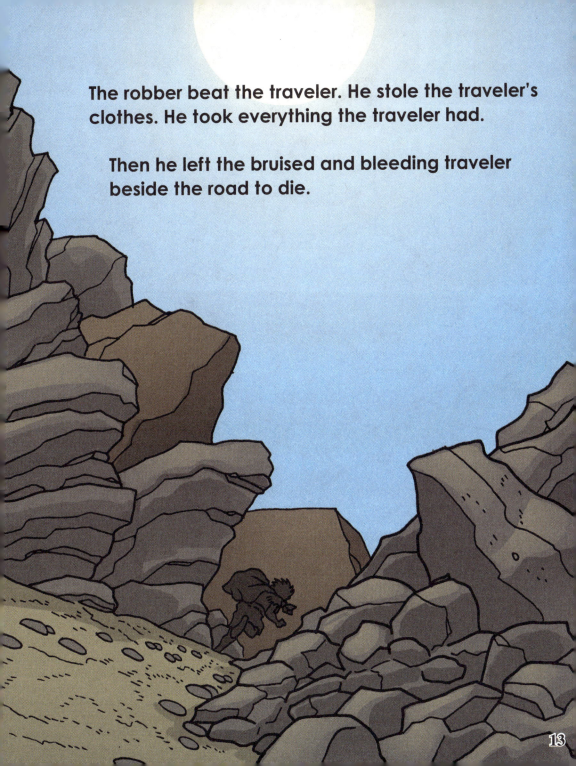

The robber beat the traveler. He stole the traveler's clothes. He took everything the traveler had.

Then he left the bruised and bleeding traveler beside the road to die.

Soon, a priest came along. He saw the wounded traveler lying beside the road.

The priest could have helped him. He should have helped him. But he didn't want to touch the traveler. He passed by on the other side of the road.

Next a Levite came along. He saw the wounded traveler lying beside the road.

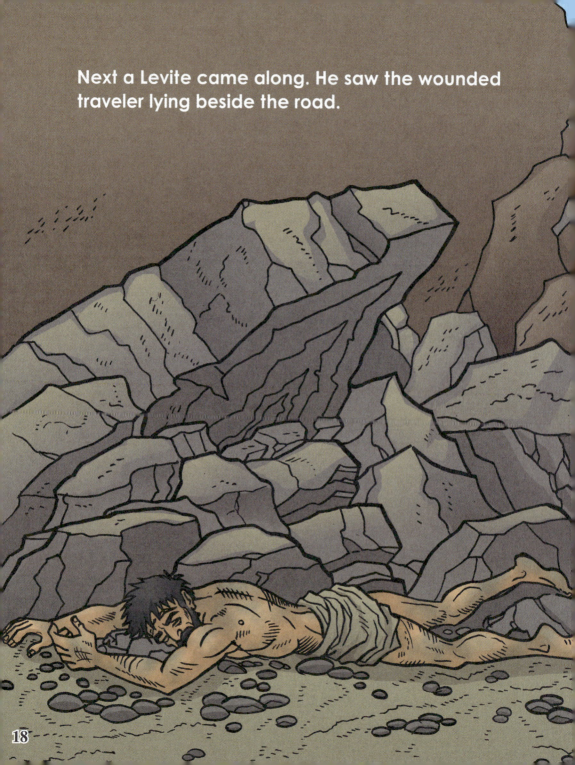

The Levite could have helped him. He should have helped him. But he didn't want to touch the traveler, either. He passed by on the other side of the road, too.

Then a Samaritan came along. Samaritans and Jews did not like each other. They had nothing to do with each other.

But when the Samaritan saw the wounded traveler lying beside the road, he felt sorry for him.

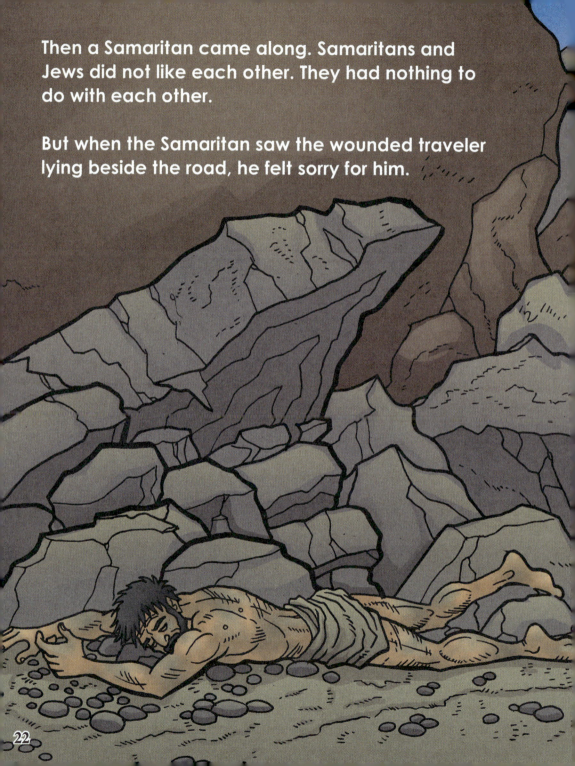

23

The Samaritan knew the traveler might die if he did not get help right away. He didn't care if the traveler was a Jew or a Samaritan.

So the Samaritan began to help.

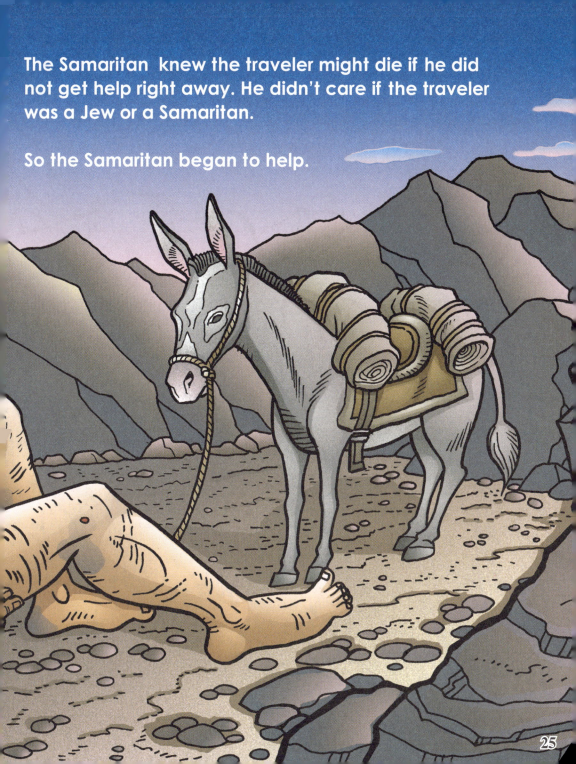

The Samaritan cleaned the traveler's wounds. He put medicine on the wounds and bandaged them.

Then he gently helped the wounded traveler onto his donkey and headed for town.

When he reached town, the Samaritan took the wounded traveler to the nearest inn. He gave the innkeeper some money. He made the innkeeper promise to take care of the traveler until he was well again.

When Jesus finished this story, he asked the lawyer, "Which of these three was a neighbor to the traveler who was beaten and robbed?"

The lawyer replied, "The one who was kind to him."